T0115364

HEAR OUR MUSIC

Tim & April Bell Mix Tape 2014,
by Tim Bell & April Bell
It's A New Day, by Tim Bell & April Bell
Forever Love, by Tim Bell & April Bell
On Apple Music, Amazon Music, Reverb Nation,
Iheart Radio, Google Play, and YouTube, etc.

OUR BOOKS

"*How to Play Piano Quick*", by Tim Bell
And "Forever Love, How to Stay Married Without
Losing Your Mind", by Tim and April Bell

AVAILABLE AT

Author House, Google Play Books, Apple
Books, Barns & Noble, and Audible

FOREVER LOVE

How to Stay Married Without Losing Your Mind

TIM and APRIL BELL

authorHOUSE®

AuthorHouse™
1663 Liberty Drive
Bloomington, IN 47403
www.authorhouse.com
Phone: 833-262-8899

Published by AuthorHouse 09/18/2020

ISBN: 978-1-6655-0017-3 (sc)
ISBN: 978-1-6655-0023-4 (e)

Library of Congress Control Number: 2020917764

Print information available on the last page.

Any people depicted in stock imagery provided by Getty Images are models, and such images are being used for illustrative purposes only. Certain stock imagery © Getty Images.

This book is printed on acid-free paper.

Because of the dynamic nature of the Internet, any web addresses or links contained in this book may have changed since publication and may no longer be valid. The views expressed in this work are solely those of the author and do not necessarily reflect the views of the publisher, and the publisher hereby disclaims any responsibility for them.

CONTENTS

PRAYER

Our Father which art in heaven,
Hallowed be thy name.
Thy kingdom come, thy will be
done in earth, as it is in heaven.
Give us this day, our daily bread.
And forgive us our debts, as
we forgive our debtors.
And lead us not into temptation,
but deliver us from evil:
For thine is the kingdom, and
the power and the glory,
For ever and ever.
Amen.

DEDICATION

**We'd like to dedicate this book to our
three beautiful daughters, Melody Bell,
Michele Bell and Marcia Bell.**

Dear daughters. Always follow your hearts and trust God before men. He will not lead you astray. Even when you get off course, He is there to bring you back with love and give you wisdom. We pray that each of you be happy, successful, and blessed in every area of your lives. We both love you very much and want the best for you. Getting married is easy, staying married is where the real work begins. But, when both of you are willing to work at it, you can have that forever love.

To our Mothers, Lillian Howard, and Martha Bell

Although we are thankful for our fathers, we are very grateful to the both of you. We learned many life lessons with your love, support, and guidance through it all. We applaud you for being successful and victorious mothers and women of God. We miss you dearly but will never forget the things you taught us. Continue to Rest in Paradise.

Sincerely, your son and daughter, Tim and April Bell

INTRODUCTION

Hello, Tim and I would like to share some of our personal experiences and helpful tools with you that helped us make a lasting marriage-relationship and a happy home. We are not experts on successful marriages or relationships. This is our story and not a substitution for professional marriage, mental health, or psychiatric counseling. Our family, friends and co-workers were a part of our inspiration for writing this book. They frequently asked us how we stayed married for so long? What is the secret? We give God all the Glory for our blessed union.

We are two multi-talented individuals who fell in love after meeting at Lincoln Junior Senior High School. We were both born and raised in Milwaukee, Wisconsin. We started a band called April Madness Showband in the early 1980's. We got married and baptized together in 1987. We have three beautiful daughters and were Foster Parents for two of my great nephews and two lovely teen girls.

In the early 1990's we recorded and published our first two gospel albums on cassette tape called, "Changed" and "I'm Free". In 2014 we had those cassettes converted to a CD called, "Tim and April Bell Mix Tape", and we produced "It's a New Day" album in 2015. We are currently working on a Love Music album for this book called, "Forever Love".

Tim was voted as the Pastor of a beautiful family Church in our hometown for ten years called Showers of Blessings, under the direction of Founder-Pastor Mother Hattie Foster-Hall. I am also an ordained Minister of the Gospel and a Music Evangelist. We also have experience in marriage counseling.

In 2007 we started a music school called Grace Music Conservatory, which is now known as Grace Music Academy. We teach piano from our book called "How to Play Piano Quick", lead and bass guitar, drums, voice and more. Tim produces music for us and others in our private studio, along with Music Business Training sessions. In this book, Tim and I will share more of our personal stories and how we met. We hope you enjoy this and find some helpful tools and information that will bless you and your relationship.

TIM SAYS

Growing up with my mother, grandmother, two younger sisters, two older sisters, and one older brother, I thought that I never wanted to get married. My grandmother taught us how to cook, clean, and take care of our home.

Thanks to my grandmother, Henrietta Stramler, I learned how to do plumbing, windows, painting, and gardening, etc. So, I really did not think that I would ever need a woman or wife.

I grew up working in our family bar, where my mother taught me how to run a business and about entrepreneurship. My father left us when I was about nine years old. He left my mom with six children and a whole bunch of bills. My mother Martha Bell was a strong woman who never gave up. Despite all the challenges, she raised us up in a happy home.

I thank God every day for my family, especially my mother and grandmother. They loved us hard and taught me many life lessons, while allowing me to find my own way. They never stopped caring and praying for me until they left this earth.

The older guys taught and misguided me. They said that a relationship was a waste of time and it was more about getting paid than finding love. But, in my teenage years, I ran across this young lady on the bridge going home from school, who seemed quite interesting. She really gave me a different insight on what a relationship could be. It was not about manipulating a person, but more about uniting and building each other up. My first impression of her was, "you got potential". She is my music super star and I am her biggest fan and supporter.

As we grew together and started thinking about having a family, I made up my mind that if we had children, I would never leave my wife and children.

Because of my history, I believe it is important to stay in your children's lives and do your parental duties to provide for them and help them to be the best they can be. As a man you should love yourself and be the best you can be. Do not be too proud to ask for help and remember that you are never too young, old, or important to learn something new every day.

APRIL SAYS

Growing up in a single parent home with my beautiful mother, three sisters and brother, I always dreamed of one day getting married and having children (as most girls do). I learned to keep house and cook too. I was also very smart and involved with activities in and out of school.

When I met my soulmate on that bridge, walking home from school, I did not know exactly what was going on. When we got to my house, I pretended that it was my aunt's house. I ran up the stairs and told my sisters to come look out the window. I saw him more clearly from that view. He had such a cute nose, and a beautiful spark in his big brown eyes. My downstairs neighbor, whose nickname was Fats, gave him my phone number on one of his homework folders. Somehow, he lost his folder, but one of his younger sisters remembered it by heart, thanks Renee. We began a slow- paced friendship as teens and after twelve years of friendship, over thirty years of marriage and 3 beautiful daughters, he still has that spark in his eyes.

I am very grateful to God for every minute, hour, and day of our journey. It has not always been easy, I could not always have my way but, if I could choose again, he would still be my choice and I hope he feels the same about me.

Although we lived close by each other, we may have never met if his mom had not forced him to go to her alma mater Lincoln Jr Sr High School.

Looking back, I know that you never know where your soulmate is coming from, but it is so amazing how these things work out.

I spent a lot of time getting to know my husband before we took important steps. I still think it is very important not to jump into sex before truly getting to know a person. I also spent time getting to know his family during holidays, church and just hanging out with him.

We would love for you to have little activities and/or discussions after each chapter.

Here is the first one, have fun!

Activity/Discussion: Talk about your families where you grew up. Share somethings you have learned from them.

CHAPTER 1

KNOW WHO YOU ARE

APRIL SAYS

Before considering marriage, Tim and I wanted to stress the importance of knowing who you are. You may already be married or have been married in the past. But it is never too late to get to know yourself. Knowing yourself means understanding your passions, desires, strengths, weaknesses, fears, dreams, likes, and dislikes, tolerances and limitations.

Part of knowing yourself is knowing your purpose. As we grow from childhood into puberty and into adulthood, we have heard, seen, learned and experienced a lot from our guardians, family, friends, and teachers. Some experiences were not necessarily all good, and neither were some of our behavior.

It does not matter if you were raised in a happy or abusive, rich, or poor environment, it is a part of your history. It should not be ignored but accepted for what it was. Part of knowing ourselves is dealing with our past and healing from any bad situations and finding a healthy balance in life. You have probably heard the saying, "it's not good to live in the past, but learn from it."

You cannot change the past but, know that you are wonderfully and beautifully made. So, love yourself and do not accept abuse from anyone. Know that if you have childhood scars, or anger problems, such things can affect your relationships, work, and life. Please consider seeking professional counseling.

TIM SAYS

Here is an important check list to
help you know who you are.

Activity/Discussion:

1. Sit down in a quiet space and meditate, listen to your heart. You will not get to know yourself without having personal time.
2. Realize who you are, not who you want to be, nor try to be somebody else.
3. Find out what you are good at, and what you are not good at.
4. What are you passionate about?
5. Get some feedback from other people about what you are good at.
6. Assess your relationships. What are their purposes?

CHAPTER 2

LOVE YOURSELF
(SELF-LOVE)

TIM SAYS

Let's talk about <u>Self-Love</u> because, to know you is to love you. Self-love is a pre-requisite for a good life and a healthy relationship. It is also a very positive concept involving the practice of several self-enhancing qualities of thinking, feeling, and acting towards yourself. If you do not love yourself, you cannot love anybody else because, you cannot give what you do not have. Parents, please tell your children that you love them every day. Seek therapy if you are in need of emotional healing.

Dr. Antonio Burrello describes self-love as a process consisting of 6 distinct components where the person acts as both the doer and the object relating to one's self.

1. Self-attachment: Feeling attached to yourself, physically and mentally.
2. Self-affection: Feeling at peace with who and what you are, along with enjoying your own company.

3. Positive Self-regard: Unconditionally accepting yourself despite successes, failures, or status.

4. Self-worth: Belief that your life is a valued possession and trusting your ability to respond to your needs.

5. Self-knowing: The ability to see yourself from the outside, to listen to, know and understand yourself.

6. Self-caring: Your behaviors aimed at maintaining your health and personal welfare. So, take the time to get to know yourself and become your own best friend. See examples below.

If you are trying to lose weight, you know you need to eat healthy and exercise. If you must get up early in the morning for work or school, self-love will have you to go to bed early and get plenty of rest. If you want to have good grades in school/college, do your homework, study for your tests, go to bed early, and get up early enough to have some breakfast, and if you are aware you have high blood pressure, do not eat pork chops every day.

APRIL SAYS

If we can love ourselves then we can love others. If we do not love ourselves, it is like rejecting what God has made. Think of the love between a parent and a child. To know love is to know how to love. And if no one else loves you, God does, and He created it so that we can have life. What the world needs now is love sweet love.

It's human nature to be our own worst critics. But do not beat up on yourself about learning, growing, and making mistakes. It is all a part of life's lessons as a human being.

You want to dream and have goals and challenge yourself to meet your goals. You want to create the best life for yourself and others.

Discipline is necessary but so is being patient and not prideful. Just as our Maker loves us, we need to love ourselves through the good and bad experiences, failures, and victories.

God does not make mistakes and you are valuable, and you are a winner. When you fall, get back up because we are all learning how to walk this walk!

Love yourself enough not to let others treat you badly or abuse you in any way. Do not stay around people who make you feel bad about yourself.

Sometimes we are around people who are rude to us in life, for example, at school and workplaces. That is temporary, we do not have to live with those people. Be sure to stand up for yourself and continue to practice walking in love.

As I look in the mirror, I am almost 60 years old now. I still love myself. I want to tell everyone, especially my children and grandchildren that if you want to have a beautiful life, to take good care of yourself, exercise and keep learning. Follow your dreams, start businesses, save money, and have multiple streams of income.

Activity/Discussion: Love and forgive yourself. Write positive changes that you need to make to create a better and healthier life.

CHAPTER 3

WHAT MAKES YOU HAPPY?

TIM & APRIL SAYS

What Makes You Happy can be summed up in one word, *"Progress"*.

We know material things and advancements are exciting for a moment but what makes you happy in the long run is when you can see progress.

Progress takes moving forward with positive, consistent choices and persistency to work toward the life you really want. You love getting up in the morning when you know you are moving forward, growing, contributing, impacting, and/or serving others in your life. Progress on our goals lead to a win-win situation if we can just *put in the work.*

When you know what makes you happy, you will find that its much easier to know what you want in a relationship/marriage and partner.

This could be a very difficult question to answer by many people. If you are having difficulty deciding what makes you happy, flip the script and list the things that make you unhappy or stressed. Nobody is going to be perfect but, to have the right mate to spend the rest of your life with is going to take time and investigating before entering marriage. No one is responsible for your happiness; you must go back to knowing and loving yourself. Your partner is not responsible for your happiness but when you have a loving and considerate partner, they will add to and encourage your happiness.

If you are dating or in a relationship where you are having all kinds of problems, you may need to re-evaluate whether this is the person you want to spend the rest of your life with. You should be considerate and respectful of each other's feelings, likes, dislikes, desires, dreams, and goals. If not, you are not going to be happy.

Take some time to get to know a perspective partner and figure out if you want and/or like the same things.

Activity/Discussion: Make a list of what makes you happy, your dreams and goals. Share with group/partner, listen and support others when they share.

CHAPTER 4

GET YOURSELF TOGETHER

TIM SAYS

Getting Yourself Together and/or getting your life in order is part of self-love. Please understand that you need to get yourself together for you! Accomplishing this is not to become some type of whipping boy for your woman.

Make sure you focus on your financial stability, your personal hygiene, your physical appearance, your transportation and having your own house will make your life better and make you more attractive to women. Do not go by any list that women make, saying what you got to have for them to accept you.

Let us talk about five ways to be more attractive to women. This list is not written for women by women, this list is written for men by men.

1. Competence-The ability to do something efficiently and/or successfully.
2. Body Image-The subjective picture or mental image of one's body.
3. Remove all the zeroes from your life. Get rid of all the negative people around you that are taking

from you and not adding nothing to you. Those that are giving you bad advice, but never having anything positive to say.

4. Be a lifelong learner. Do not be afraid to admit when you don't know something. Be willing to find out, search and research, because when you seek, you shall find, ask and it shall be given, knock and the door will be opened to you.

5. Do not allow drugs and alcohol to rule your life.

Dear women. There are only three things that men really need.

1. Respect, 2. Food and 3. Sex.

APRIL SAYS

There were certain things expected of us by our parents when we were children. At home, we had to go to bed at a certain time, get up at a certain time, get dressed, eat breakfast and off to school.

At school we were expected to listen to and respect our teachers, follow the rules, and learn. We were also taught and expected to respect all our elders.

I followed these guidelines into adulthood and taught them to my children.

Before I had children, I had to get myself together by

graduating from high school, going to college, getting a job, getting my driver's license, buying my clothes, getting a place to live, and paying bills. We taught our children the same things that we learned and things that were expected.

Most people came up the same way but not all. If you were not taught these things when you were growing up, it's not too late; you need to go back and get your ducks in a row.

Tim hit on some things that are important for men to have together. Those things like competence, body image and so on are important for us ladies too.

I do not think that women want a whipping boy or a push-over man. Women want a man whom they can respect, look up to, confide in and feel safe with. We want a man who is a leader not a follower and knows he doesn't know it all. We want a partner who has dreams and goals but also able to support ours. Please don't come asking for a date or marriage if you have a lot of unsolved issues ladies and gentlemen. For example, if you know you're a drug addict, alcoholic, an abuser, or unemployed, get yourself together, ask for help, keep it real!

Tim mentioned three things that a man really needs from a perspective partner. Ladies need those three things too. What else do we expect and/or need?

Activity/Discussion: Talk about what qualities you would like your life partner to have. Share what qualities and accomplishments that you bring with you.

CHAPTER 5

DATING AND MEETING NEW PEOPLE

APRIL SAYS

You may be wondering why we are discussing dating in this book about marriage. We believe that dating comes before something as permanent as marriage, and it is a great start to building a great relationship.

Having a goal for dating will help you find the results that you are looking for. Some people act like they want a relationship but do not want to compromise or take other people's cares and desires into consideration. Some people just want to hang out and be friends with benefits. Know what you want and do not settle for less.

Physical attraction gets the ball rolling in wanting to know someone. It goes hand in hand with having good chemistry with one another. That just mean that you feel comfortable around one another. But remember that you cannot judge a book by its cover. Some people may look like they have it all together on the outside but, when you get to know them, it may be quite the opposite. On the other hand, a person can look very nerdy but, have wonderful qualities, life skills, personality, and morals.

Do not hesitate to excuse yourself quickly from an acquaintance whom you were attracted to when you realize that you have nothing in common, and/or you have totally different beliefs and backgrounds. Do not tolerate disrespect and rude behavior. It is much easier to quit while you are ahead. If you start seeing a lot of red flags, you do not want to go in too deep nor stay too long with the wrong person. Follow your heart and use your brain. Trust must be earned. There's comfort and strength when you meet someone with similar goals, morals, beliefs, and standards.

My husband Tim and I have similar beliefs and standards. We both have close family ties, we both believe in God, we both love music and live performance, and we love to keep our home and workspaces clean and organized. On the other hand, it is true that opposites attract. We are opposite in many ways but balance each other out. I am the calm and he is the storm but, sometimes we switch.

Women want joy, peace, contentment, romance and more. We want to be that special piece of jewelry that a man loves and cherish.

Some women say it takes more than one man to make them happy. They would have one that has plenty of money, one with plenty of stamina in the bedroom, a great listener, one that likes to shop, one that likes to stay home and cook, one that likes to praise God and one that likes to wine and dine them. Consider yourself blessed like me to meet, date, and share your life with someone who does all these things. It is possible!

My husband would like to share some helpful and interesting information with men, about women while dating. I may not totally agree, but he convinced me that these things are not mentioned to put women down nor to make men distrust them. He wanted to share this information so that men will pay more attention to their partners and satisfy their needs.

TIM SAYS

I believe that everyone should be running towards their spiritual and personal development and purpose. If a person can run with you and support you while on your journey, then maybe you have something to work with.

Just remember that, according to scripture, not everyone is intended to be married. In the book of Corinthians, Paul wrote that some people just need to be single so they can focus on their mission and not worry about trying to please a husband or a wife.

For centuries, men have been known for being players in relationships. But women are very good at it too, if not better.

According to Richard Cooper's website called, "Entrepreneurs in Cars, Become the Best Version of

Yourself"; here are 5 things that men need to know about women.

1. Women "monkey-branch" switch mates faster than you think.
2. Women Date Up(hypergamy). They may not be attracted to you nor care for you and will leave you no matter what you can give. Money cannot buy love.
3. Women date more people at one time(simultaneously) than you do.
4. Women get bored faster than men in a relationship.
5. Women cheat as much as men but mostly when ovulating.

When dating, we have been told to be ourselves but, more importantly, men and women should be the best version of themselves.

Meeting a new people can be very exciting but let the honeymoon stage pass and see how you are together in real life situations. Keep communication open.

Activity/Discussion: Have you had some bad dating experiences? What qualities are you looking for in a life partner? What are some red flags or deal breakers for you to stop dating a person?

CHAPTER 6

BE SURE BEFORE
YOU SAY "I DO"

APRIL SAYS

It's pretty easy to go somewhere and get married. You can even have your family and friends involved but you have not truly gotten to know each other! It will be very much worth your time and happiness, to participate in *Pre-marital Counseling. Get to know and share your likes and dislikes, your dreams and goals, expectations, and beliefs in a life-partner. You do not want to be two fools with a misunderstanding (thanks Bob Johnson).*

So, date-date-date and have as long of an engagement as you like. What is the rush?

Wikipedia says that marriage is the legally or formally recognized union of 2 people as partners in a personal relationship.

Marriage is also called Matrimony or Wedlock, where spouses establishes rights and obligations between them, their children, and in-laws.

Let's also look at what the Holy Bible says about marriage. The Apostle Paul, a special messenger of Jesus Christ, speaks to husbands and wives in the New Testament's book of

Ephesians, Chapter 5:21-33. We are not going to write all the verses referred here, but I'd like to share my favorite parts.

In verse 21, of the Amplified Bible, Paul starts by saying: "Be subject to one another out of reverence for Christ" (the Messiah, the Anointed One). And it ends in verse 33 saying: "However, let each man (without exception) love his wife as (being in a sense) his very own self; and let the wife see that she respects and reverences her husband" [that she notices him, regards him, honors him, prefers him, venerates him and esteems him; and that she defers to him, praises him and loves and admires him exceedingly].

The word of God has been such a blessing in our marriage. God wants us to be victorious and have joy and peace in our lives and marriages. When two people come together, let it be about love. Include the greatest love of all in your relationships, marriage and in your life. No matter what you go through, you win.

TIM SAYS

In the book of Ephesians, Paul gives twice as much instruction to the husband to love his wife than he gave to the wife to submit. The husband should:

1. Be willing to sacrifice everything for her.
2. Make her well-being of primary importance, and
3. Care for her as he cares for his own body.

17

If he does this, there is no woman that will be afraid nor hesitant of submitting to him.

As the Lord gave everything for the church, the husband is to give everything to the wife, but he does not lose. Just like the church is presented back to Christ as an unspotted, unwrinkled, and unblemished gift, is the way the wife comes back to him. So, in the same token, if you give everything to your wife, do not think you're going to lose because she is presented back to you as the precious gift that you have for yourself.

Understanding this is how you can have the assurance of a great return and stay in a marriage without losing your mind. Because real love is a beautiful thing.

-True Story-

After my wife conceived our third child, I was concerned about her health. I considered her body as my own. I was in the labor and delivery room with our first two daughters and saw what women went through to deliver a baby. This made me support her decision that three children were enough. Even though I did not get a boy out of the deal, I thank God for our three healthy daughters. My wife's health and wellbeing are just as important as my own.

Activity/Discussion: Discuss your thoughts on the definitions of marriage and Ephesians 5:21-33. Are both of you in agreement with what is expected. Why and/or why not?

CHAPTER 7

THE MARRIED COUPLE

APRIL SAYS

Congratulations if you are married! Even if it has only been for a few hours, days, weeks, months, or many years, you two have become one! Yet, you are still individuals with your own personalities (which you should not allow anyone to change), flaws, and responsibilities.

In the beginning of our book, Tim and I shared information about getting yourself together, being the best, you can be and expecting the best in a life partner. We also talked about getting to know yourself and possible life partner before you say, "I do". These things should not be overlooked nor ignored if you want your marriage to last for a lifetime. You want that forever-love. Friendship and communication are very important to a happy marriage. You will have peace, joy, unity and more.

Tim and I have been married for over 30 years now and it seem like the years just flew by so fast! I look back to see with these things operating in our marriage, God brought us through the good, bad, beautiful, and ugly times.

It is not always going to be blue skies and apple pie.

In the hard times, be there for one another. I heard a great phrase lately that said, "when problems come, we're not against each other, we are against the problem". The problem could be an illness, so go against it together. The problem could be the loss of a loved one. Be patient, supportive and understanding and let your partner exercise their right to grieve.

You will find that in certain circumstances that your partner and/or you may be extra emotional and more sensitive than usual. It may seem like they are losing their minds or blowing up for a small situation, but it is all a part of grieving and stress. Be forgiving and do not be ashamed to cry on each other's shoulders. It never seems to be a good time for sickness, nor death or accidents but, they are a part of life that we can get through better, together.

TIM SAYS

I have a few points to share that has helped April and me in our relationship. The focus of my points is to strengthen the unity and bond of two becoming one.

1. **<u>Think of some ways to make the other person happy</u>**.

Husbands can do the dishes or laundry without having to be asked.

In our early years of marriage, when our children were very small, I took our clothes to the laundry mat, to wash and fold them while she stayed home with the children. Also, after all three girls were in school and my wife started working, I had time to make the beds and straighten up the house before I started my workday. Eventually, the Lord delivered us from public transportation and laundry facilities. The point is, no matter how big or small the gesture, be willing to do things to make your partner happy on purpose. It will pay off in the long run.

2. **Pay compliments to each other.**

    Do not always find fault or criticize your partner. Pump them up with positive words that make them feel valuable.

3. **Express thanks to one another.**

    When your partner cleans the house, cooks, and pay bills and more, say thank you. You may feel like they are supposed to do certain things but it's always good to let them know that you appreciate what they do.

4. **Apologize when you screw up.**

    Sometimes guys can be so insensitive. We may unintentionally offend or annoy our partner. We need to try to understand how they feel and apologize for any offense, and not let our ego nor pride stand in the way.

5. **Exercise regular physical contact with your partner**.

Small gestures of physical affection mean the world to some people and makes them feel loved every day.

Activity/Discussion: Discuss where you are now in your marriage. Is it what you expected? If not, each of you write down 3 things that you love about your marriage and 3 things you would like to improve.

CHAPTER 8

ENJOYING LIFE TOGETHER

APRIL SAYS

Tim and I want to share topics that we believe helped us keep a long lasting and happy marriage. We believe that couples should find ways to enjoy life together. Sharing some of the same interests have helped.

Tim and I make music together. We both loved music and performing since we were children. We have been playing music together before our marriage began, and we are not done writing, performing, recording, publishing, and teaching music together. We also raised our children together, share our circle of family and friends together (especially for holidays and birthdays), worship the Lord together, cheer for our favorite sports teams together and keep up our home together. I am so grateful that my husband stuck it out with me to raise our children. We both looked up to and respected our mothers enough to want to make them proud of us by being good and responsible parents for their grandchildren.

Enjoying life together is not just about partying and taking big trips, but about making your everyday life enjoyable. Meeting as teens, I always looked forward to the day when we did not have to say "goodbye" or "see you tomorrow". You know you have a strong possibility for a marriage partner when you want to live under the same roof.

I must admit that romance and fun came so natural in our first 20 years of marriage but became more challenging as we got older. When you start getting up in age, like in your 50's, you start looking at your life differently and re-evaluating what you want. You start thinking about retirement and looking at your goals and thinking about what kind of legacy you want to leave behind, and how to make the world a better place. These things should be important to young couples and single people as well. The conclusion is, no matter how important finances, success and ministry are, if you want your love life to stay significant, thriving and hot, you both have to take out time for fun and romance because it is definitely a part of enjoying life together.

This became more challenging in our 50s, compared to when we were younger. I recently retired from my job and laid my beautiful mother to rest after her 82nd birthday. I realized that even though I had retired and going through grievance from the loss of my mother, I needed to stay active to remain healthy. Also, Tim wears several hats in business. The more successful business gets, sometimes means less fun and quality time together.

Life, loss, work, and health challenges can affect relationships and marriage. But the love and patience we have for each other, the trust we have in God for every need and concern and taking care of our health gave us some of the necessary tools we needed to keep enjoying life together.

Here are some other tools we use that may be helpful to you too:

1. Keep a positive state of mind and attitude.
2. Google positive self-motivation quotes and videos, and
3. Search for interesting and helpful books about marriage and relationships.

One book that has been a help to us lately is "The 5 Love Languages-The Secret to Love That Lasts" by Gary Chapman. You never stop learning about yourself nor your partner. When you think you got them down pact, you learn something new. We took Gary Chapman's "5 Love Language Quiz"! My Love language profile for couples says: I like to receive gifts, physical touch, words of affirmation, acts of service and quality time. Tim likes physical touch, quality time, words of affirmation, acts of service and receiving gifts.

This was both fun and interesting. And I think it is really important to know each other well enough to make sure that both of you are still happy and deal with any issues that are making you unhappy in your marriage. It is also important to be truly present when you are in the same space instead of being there but not there.

Some couples live in the same house and hardly ever talk, especially with the competition of the TV, social media, and video games. None of those things are more important than our relationship. There is a time for everything under the sun. And our significant others should be our top priority. Tim and I are continuing to enjoy life together by making sure that we are good mentally, physically, and spiritually. Also, by doing things that we enjoy, and fulfilling more purpose.

TIM SAYS

Enjoying married life together is not just one big event. You cannot put it all in one big experience because life is to be lived moment by moment. As April and I were growing in our marriage, we were doing music together. We were having lots of rehearsals, having fun doing gigs, plenty of love making, and just living life together. Do not forget to always take some personal time for yourself.

Marriage is not about finding the person you can live with; it is about finding the person that you cannot live without.

I remember back when our first daughter was born, we had a band called April Madness Showband. We used to play at various locations in the city of Milwaukee. I can remember being at rehearsal and putting Melody to sleep in my bass guitar case, wrapped in her little blanket. She got her name from some of my favorite lyrics in one of Bootsy Collins' (an American musician, singer, and songwriter. Rising to prominence with James Brown in the early 1970's, and later with Parliament-Funkadelic, Collins's driving bass guitar and humorous vocals established him as one of the leading names in funk.) songs that said, "your name should be Melody baby, cause your personality is uh so melodic".

The same year that Melody turned one year old, we got married. After signing the license at our Pastor Mother Price's home, we had a beautiful celebration dinner with my big sister Eleanor, brother in-law Virge, and cousin, Evangelist Rosa Flood. After dinner we enjoyed a walk together in downtown, Milwaukee. I did not have a quarter to my name, but I was just as happy as I could be. The point I am getting to is, you do not have to have a whole lot of money to be happy and enjoy life together, but at the same time it's needed. So, enjoy saving, budgeting, and making plans for special dates.

The following month, November 14, 1987, we had a beautiful wedding ceremony and catered reception with our families and friends. Although we had over ten years of friendship, our honeymoon stage was wonderful. But do not be deceived to think that the honeymoon stage is going to last forever.

When that honeymoon feeling is gone and you come back down to earth, you are still going to have to do the hard work of listening and learning how to listen to each other.

You should also learn the different types of ways that your partner understands about being loved. We believe that everyone has a "love tank". The "Love Tank" is talked about in Day 1 of Gary Chapman's "5 Love Languages 7 Day Devotional for Him and Her".

April and I keep each other's love tanks full by greeting each other with a kiss, giving compliments, saying I love you, supporting each other's interests and activities, gift giving, intimacy, romance and more.

Activity/Discussion: What do you like doing together as a married couple?

If you do not have a date-night, choose a day of the week that you both can spend and enjoy together. It does not have to always be in the evening, and it does not have to be every week, but stick to your plans.

Finally, feel free to go to Gary Chapmans website: 5lovelanguages.com and take the 5 Love Languages Quiz and check out the 7 Day Devotionals.

CHAPTER 9

SUPPORT ONE ANOTHER

TIM SAYS

We found a couple of definitions for the word
<u>SUPPORT</u>: (1) To sustain or withstand (weight,
pressure, strain, etc. without giving way; serve as
a prop for. (2) To undergo or endure especially
with patience or submission; tolerate.

This may seem like a lot of work to do for one another but,
it is not that hard when you love someone. So, do not be
overwhelmed or throw in the towel.

Being supportive in a relationship brings benefits
to both people. Here are some important ways to be
supportive that have helped April and I in our marriage
that could also be beneficial to your relationship.

1. **Be respectful to your partner's feelings**.

If your partner is dealing with a disappointment, a
problematic situation or grief, let them know that you
are available to talk anytime, no matter how late at night
it may be.

2. **Listen intently to your partner.**

Make sure you understand what they are saying. Repeat the concern or request back to him or her to make sure you are on the same page. Do not interject your own feelings into what they are saying, and do not try to fix it, just listen.

3. **Communicate in a loving tone.**

The Holy Bible says: "Through love and kindness have I drawn thee". Your conversation will be accepted better without harsh tones and bad attitudes.

Using a loving tone of voice demonstrates that you really care and shows your partner that you are concerned and supportive.

4. **Give each other space and trust.** Although it is important to do things together often in your marriage, it's just as important to have some alone time. Giving him or her space and trust is another way of being supportive. Spend some time in your Man Cave and She Shed.

APRIL SAYS

As a couple you may not be interested in participating in everything together. Nevertheless, it is important to show support. My husband wanted to teach music, preach, and do home improvement. Even though these were not my dreams, as his wife I support him 100%. We have similar likes and goals, but even when they are different, we encourage and support one another.

It makes any task in life easier if the person you live with and love shows support and not resistance.

If your partner decided to get a college degree, there is no reason to feel jealous nor to suddenly think that they think that they are better than you. Some ways to show support is to help them get to class, be considerate of some study time needed at home, and celebrate every good grade. You can also help more around the house or with meals sometimes.

As a wife, when my husband was filling in as Pastor of a church, I made sure I was there and helped in any way that I could. I made sure to give him time to study for sermons and we made time for our church family and fellowshipping.

As CEO of Grace Music Academy, I help with administrative and clerical work, music recitals, creating programs, performance, and music lessons.

We support each other with our daughters, our parents and any family matters that go on in both of our families, and our families supports us.

Everything that I love to do and have, my husband supports 100% and if he sees anything that could be a problem, he is right there to help.

Sometimes we do not know how to be supportive

of our partners when they are going through a difficult time or when they are going into new territories. Do not hesitate to seek out and google information on topics of supporting one another.

Activity/Discussion: How do you and your partner support each other? Share where you could use more support at this time.

CHAPTER 10

CELEBRATE YOUR UNION AND DIFFERENCES

It may seem corny or carnal but, to me, celebrating your union and other special days keeps your marriage and relationship exciting and fresh.

Google dictionary says, "to celebrate is to observe a day or commemorate an event with ceremonies or festivities. To praise widely or to present to a widespread and favorable public notice". I guess that is why we like to share pictures, announce special days and anniversaries on Facebook and other social media outlets.

Even though Tim and I have been married for over 30 years, our wedding anniversary, birthdays, and romantic holidays are still important. Just because we have been together a long time and have gotten older does not mean that we no longer have the need and desire for compliments, gifts, flowers, dates, and the celebration of oneness(sex)!

Back in our twenties and thirties it seemed that we had more time and energy for romance. In our forties and fifties, we gave more time and energy to work, ministry, and business. That is why I love special anniversaries and holidays, because they remind us to take out time to celebrate our union. We have a special wedding song, like most couples do and every anniversary we choose another song (old or new) to help us celebrate our special day.

Celebrating our union also requires us to *celebrate our differences*. It is true that opposites attract. It is also true that we should have things in common with our life partner like values, and beliefs. We do not need a carbon copy of ourselves. We need someone who completes what is lacking in us, someone who compliments us and makes us better.

Sometimes the things that attract you to your partner are the very things that start to annoy you, lol! That driven spark in Tim's eyes that helped draw me to him is still there but, when he is working too much inside or out of our home, it would get on my last nerve. And he was attracted to me for my gorgeous looks, fashionable style of dressing, and musical talents. Yet, I am sure that my love for shopping, going to the salon and not being as driven in the business world and music as he is, sometimes gets on his last nerve. We must love one another enough to allow the other to change, evolve and grow. Even though there have been changes, we have not grown apart.

Speaking of growing apart, sometimes your differences and interests can pull you away from one another. Spending a lot of time working to be more successful for a better quality of life can seem more important than your relationship.

So, when I am feeling lonely and/or ignored, I

communicate with him. And I expect him to do the same. If we do not feel that we can share when we are having a problem or in need of something, then it never gets solved. We cannot read each other's minds. But pay attention to body language and facial expressions for good and bad signs.

When people find differences with each other, they sometimes put one another down or insult and criticize the things that make them who they are. Complaining instead of finding time for some loving conversation about things you don't like or understand about your partner can leave them feeling discouraged or condemned.

Couples have been tested to the max lately because of the Corona Virus Pandemic (Covid-19). Households across the nation have been put on quarantine in March of 2020! This year is almost over now, and people are still contracting this deadly virus and our country's economy has been stunted terribly, almost to no return. There has also been a lot of protests because of racial injustice and killings by police all over our country.

The stresses of life are real, and people deal with them in different ways. So, in hard times and challenges of life, allow one another to live and be happy. Celebrate, embrace, and respect your differences to make your love last forever without losing your minds. Speak those things that be not as though they were. Speak life into your marriage and light into darkness. Pop open some champagne, put on some good music and dance! Celebrate your union, because life happens and the fun and romance can get left behind, but do not let it.

Activity/Discussion: When is your anniversary? How do you want to celebrate the next one? How does your differences balance the other out?

CHAPTER 11

CONFLICTS AND DISAGREEMENTS

We could not close out this book without talking about conflicts and disagreements. We are not experts in couples therapy, nor is this a certified substitution for counseling.

Every person is different and have their own likes, dislikes, and limitations to be considered when dealing with conflicts and disagreements. The ultimate goal is to come to a mutual and beneficial solution that will satisfy both partners.

Disagreements can sometimes be let go of and couples can agree to disagree, but if not, you have a conflict. There are several ways that people in relationships or even businesses deal with conflicts. Tim and I found the "5 Conflict Management Styles" shared by Mr. Thomas Kilmann, originally called, Thomas-Kilmann Conflict Mode Instrument. He has a very interesting concept in dealing with conflicts for couples. We agree with him when he said, "conflict is inevitable, but combat is optional. By embracing conflict as a part of life, you can make the most of each situation and use it as a learning opportunity."

**The 5 Conflict Management Styles are:
Collaborating, Accommodating, Avoiding,
Compromising and Competing.**

1. <u>Collaborating</u> is a win-win situation. Couples talk and find a solution that will make both parties happy. Use this style when interests, needs and beliefs of all involved need to be considered.

2. <u>Accommodating</u> is when one of you set aside your wants and needs and focus on those of the other person. This style is used when you are wrong, or you do not care about the issue as much as the other person and/or want to keep the peace. If your opinions are not respected or considered in situations, you could be in an abusive relationship.

3. <u>Avoiding</u> is to ignore the situation altogether. One or both of you steer clear of the conflict. This style is used when the conflict is meaningless, when there is not enough time to deal with it or when you are not sure how you feel about the issue.

4. <u>Compromising</u> is to try and find a way to partially satisfy both sides of the argument. Adjustments are made on both sides. This style is used when reaching a solution is more important than the solution itself, when a temporary solution is needed or when you are at a standstill.

5. <u>Competing </u>is going for the win. You take a firm stance and refuse to budge until you get what you want. You are unmoved by the perspectives of the other parties involved in the conflict. This style is used when you must stand up for yourself, your standards, rights, and your morals. This is also used when you have reached your last resort. Warning, if you always try to go for the win in every conflict, it will not be good for your relationship.

Tim also wanted to share a tool called the *Anger Number Gage*. He created this technique in marriage counseling to help couples gage their feelings of anger from 0, being not angry to 10 being very, very angry about a situation. This is a good conversation piece to create some respectful boundaries.

Couples would have to create and agree on a situation scale of 0 -10 anger gage. This helps couples not to go overboard with small situations nor below the belt.

For example:

Gages 1-5 would be for: (a) left the toilet seat up, (b) left shoes in the middle of the floor, or (c) did not flush the toilet.

Gages 5-10 would be for: (a) not spending enough time, (b) found an inappropriate text message, or (c) stole your money.

Sometimes when a person blows up about a small thing, there are other situations they are dealing with that are causing stress. We should examine our moods to find out what is really bothering us and not take out our stress on others. The most important thing when dealing with conflicts in your relationship is communicating instead of shutting down and not dealing with issues. Your goal should be to enjoy one another and have love, peace and harmony in your home, bedroom, and business.

Discussion/Activity: Discuss the 5 Conflict Management Styles. Could one or more of these be useful to you right now or in a past conflict? Try using the Anger Number Gage and create your own situations to rate.

CHAPTER 12

INTIMACY, ROMANCE
AND DESIRE

APRIL SAYS

I love to be intimate and romantical with my husband. Back in the day you could not keep us apart. We christened every room in our home!

I must admit that all sorts of things can make intimacy and romance get left in the dark. Busy lives, jobs, hobbies, age, health, and families play a major role in distracting couples from having quality time.

Some men and women think since they have been together for a long time that they do not have to put in any effort for intimacy and romance anymore. Sometimes intimacy and romance fade away without you knowing it is gone. Maybe you or your partner are not the romantic type or have other ways to show affection. One of the main reasons that people want to get married is because they want to celebrate their love for one another and let the world know about it. So, please do not allow things to become more important than the beautiful relationship you have built together.

I noticed around our 25th wedding anniversary that I was not getting a lot of romantical attention like I used to from my husband. It seemed as though the hand-holding and romantic gestures got lost in the hustle and bustle of busy days. I understand that life is real, and we are only human, but when one of you miss romance and/or intimacy in your marriage/relationship, please communicate about how much it means to you.

I did not know exactly what was going on and I could not quite explain what was missing or what I needed. Tim thought everything was fine because his love for me had not changed. But I missed romance, dating, and flirting with my husband. I was feeling lonely. Even when he was home, I still felt lonely. He would ask me what I needed him to do. The solution was not for him to sit and look in my face all day.

I thought I was losing my mind. I love, admire, appreciate, and respect my husband's great work ethic, musical skills, and extra finances, but I just felt alone. Sure, he said hello and even asked me about my day, but you could tell that he was in another world and everything else was getting more attention than me.

We knew that we did not have all the answers and there is no shame in our game so, we began to pray on it and do some research.

I found out that whining and complaining about needing more attention can run your partner away.

Focusing more attention to yourself and your interests draws him or her closer to you. But I still missed him after getting involved in more personal development.

Tim ran across an article about intimacy (into ME see), from "Black and Married with Kids", written by Aja Dorsey Jackson. And we watched some YouTube videos by Pastor Jimmy Evans who has a website called "Marriage Today". I thank God for the word intimacy! That means that you take time to go into the other person's world. That you consider their feelings, the way they like things, and their interests. It is more than a wham-bam-thank you-ma'am. It is about stopping what you are doing and visiting with them. It is like taking out the time to play with a child. You get on their level and engage in what they enjoy doing.

This fulfilled a gap that we were having and now even when he is very busy, he takes my feelings into consideration. We are both seen and heard.

After intimacy, romance comes easier. Wikipedia says *romance* is an emotional feeling of love for, or a strong attraction towards another person, and the courtship behaviors undertaken by an individual to express those overall feelings and resultant emotions.

Tim and I heard someone say that they did not recommend married couples to go into business together. We love working together and supporting one another, but sometimes it is a huge challenge. I am sure you have

heard the phrase "don't mix business with pleasure", and/
or "business before pleasure". In my world, it is hard for
a married couple to do business together if there is no
romance and pleasure in their relationship.

It can be very hard and almost impossible to work
together when you are not getting along. But respect your
business enough to come together and get it done, because
it is important and bigger than the both of you. Your
unity helps knock down any walls that stand between
you and you can communicate on other levels about any
and everything.

**Intimacy and romance do not mean
having sex or making love.**

Intimacy and romance can go on all through the
day and are very important building blocks to getting
us turned on to making love/having sex. Most times we
are not turned on if there has not been any connection
between us before bed or sex.

It is understandable that couples must work and
take care of business, children, family, and home. And
it does not take a whole long list of things to do to get
to the love connection of sex. Just a few kind words with
love and respect for one another, and some intimacy
from both sides to show that you know and care about
one another will have you in a position to get whatever
you want. I'm just saying! You both should participate

in intimacy by flirting, complimenting, touching, massaging, and showing interest in each other. Be nice and watch your attitude!

Make the right moves to get what you want ladies and gentlemen!

When you first met, you were attracted to one another, physically and sexually. Even though one or both of you wanted to eventually get to third base, you knew that first and second base could not be skipped. Through dating and conversation, you learned a lot about the other. You loved each other's smiles and tried to say and do things to see that smile as often as you could, even by being a bit humorous. You wanted to keep that attraction going, so you made sure you were wearing nice clothes, grooming, wearing nice fragrances, looking in each other's eyes, and sharing caring touches. There was a lot of intimacy, romance and conversation that led up to the celebration of oneness (sex/making love).

At the end of the day, those things are still very important and needed. Since you are married, it may not take a very long or extensive courtship to get to third base, but intimacy, romance and conversation will open the gates and lift the bridge to ecstasy.

There can be no intimacy nor romance without desire. My husband would like to share his thoughts and information about desire.

DESIRE
TIM SAYS

I think that desire is so important, and it must be communicated between partners in a relationship. In our society, the majority of the time, we try to act so nice, polite, respectful and wholesome, but we really want passion. Passion is the state of being in a temporary phase of ecstasy and euphoria. We wish that we could live in it all the time, where nothing else seems to matter. Passion is a place where everything about that person is just perfect, and you want to spend every moment with them. Every day you would spend all your money on them and make every effort necessary to make them happy. Passion feels like some type of drug. But the fact is, the high does not last forever, it cannot. Yes, it feels good but you would be so distracted and caught up with that person, and you would not get anything else done.

The loss of passion and desire is one of the main causes of sexless relationships after a few years. When we do not get our needs met, we start looking around and wondering what happened to our relationship and remembering how in love we were before.

It is important to learn to fulfill the desires of each other and to be willing to love each other and keep the love going.

I started out talking about how we were taught to be polite and not talk about our sexual desires in relationships.

This problem stemmed from how we were brought up, or even from past rejections.

When I was growing up, allowing women to vocalize about their sexual desires was frowned upon. But today, female music artists like Cardi B, Megan Thee Stallion, and Lil Kim are producing music that talks about their body parts and what they want done to them or how they like it done. Even today, some men are bashing and slut shaming them back into their little corners. Why would a woman feel comfortable sharing those feelings?

Men also have desires that they do not reveal to their partners so they miss out and can't be vulnerable because they are intimidated or ashamed, so both partners miss out on the beautiful expressions of love that could help their relationships grow.

Again, communication is the key to revealing your passions and desires that will make your love last forever. Without passion, desire and sexual fulfillment, your relationship can get boring and fall apart.

Here are 7 ways to add passion to your relationship.

1. **Plan sex**

2. **Talk about your needs**

3. **Sort out your differences**

4. **Talk about the good times**

5. **Love and care for each other**

6. **Watch romantic movies/videos together**

7. **Plan some time alone**

Activity/Discussion: What does intimacy, romance and desire mean and look like to you? What does it take to make you feel special? What do you desire sexually? Share your desires with your partner.

SUMMARY

Tim and I have had quite an experience writing this book! We have been married now for 33 years as of October 19, 2020. And we are still in love and are excited about sharing more years together. When we first started this project, we sat down together and wrote down subjects that we thought were very important to having a successful marriage. We wanted to share things that have helped us to stay married without losing our minds, with the hopes that others would be as blessed in love and marriage as we have been. We feel that it is important for every human being on earth to strive to be happy. And it starts with you, so take the wheel. We hope that you enjoyed our book and that you found some helpful tools to use, weather you are single or in a relationship, or a group. We hope that you participated in the activities and discussions listed after each chapter. Feel free to back any time and please share with others. Remember that communication is very important in every relationship because we cannot read each other's minds. Continue to live, love, laugh, work, and pray together. Take care of yourself and each other. We appreciate you and pray God's blessings on you and your forever love.

Printed in the United States
By Bookmasters